ANIMALS ON THE MOVE

IN THE WATER

WRITTEN BY
Eliza Nodes

PowerKiDS press

Published in 2026
by The Rosen Publishing Group, Inc.
2544 Clinton Street, Buffalo, NY 14224

Written by: Eliza Nodes
Edited by: Rebecca Phillips-Bartlett
Designed by: Rob Delph

All facts, statistics, web addresses, and URLs in this book were verified as valid and accurate at time of writing. No responsibility for any changes to external websites or references can be accepted by either the author or publisher.

Cataloging-in-Publication Data

Names: Nodes, Eliza.

Title: In the water / Eliza Nodes.

Description: Buffalo, New York : PowerKids Press, 2026. | Series: Animals on the move | Includes glossary and index.

Identifiers: ISBN 9781499455830 (pbk.) | ISBN 9781499455847 (library bound) | ISBN 9781499455854 (ebook)

Subjects: LCSH: Animal migration--Juvenile literature. | Animal behavior--Juvenile literature. | Adaption--Juvenile literature.

Classification: LCC QL754.N634 2026 | DDC 591.568--dc2

Printed in China

CPSIA Compliance Information: Batch #QW26PK. For further information contact Rosen Publishing at 1-800-237-9932.

PHOTO CREDITS

All images are courtesy of Shutterstock.com, unless otherwise stated. Front Cover – Mr.wutthiphat vimuktanont, Vladimir Turkenich, MuhammadIshaq0, Andrea Izzotti, Gail Johnson. 2&3 – Jade Prevost Manuel, Elvin A. Santana. 4&5 – Mozgova, Wayne Marinovich, Robert Harding Video, Ertiga88953. 6&7 – Elvin A. Santana, Bradley Olson. 8&9 – Jade Prevost Manuel, Biswanath Swain, Marti Bug Catcher. 10&11 – Jakub Rutkiewicz, Galyna Andrushko. 12&13 – Snorre Roberg, richardjohnson, Lillian Tveit. 14&15 – Jonas Gruhlke, martin_hristov. 16&17 – Perthsnap, martin_hristov. 18&19 – Andrea Izzotti, JHVEPhoto. 20&21 – Rachel Rowland, glenrichardphoto. 22&23 – TimeImage Production, Mr.wutthiphat vimuktanont, blue tang, Jody Ann, Chase D'animulls. Vectors throughout – kichikimi.

CONTENTS

Words that look like this can be found in the glossary on page 24.

WHAT IS MIGRATION?

Animals moving from one place to another is called migration. Every year, many animals migrate on land, under the ground, and through the sea and air. Some animals are always moving from place to place.

Animals that live in or on water are known as aquatic animals.

Animals migrate for lots of reasons. These include:

- To find somewhere to have their young
- To avoid difficult weather
- If their habitat is changing
- To find food and water

Let's look at some aquatic animals that migrate.

THE SEA TURTLE'S VOYAGE

There are many types of sea turtles, but they all share one thing. All sea turtles migrate and spend their lives on the move. This begins the moment they hatch from their eggs.

Newly hatched sea turtles are called hatchlings.

The hatchlings scramble down the beach to reach the water. As soon as they enter the water, they start swimming. They are starting the long journey to an underwater nursery.

Hatchlings are often snatched from the sand by birds and other predators.

Sea turtles migrate alone for thousands of miles. When it is time to have young, sea turtles migrate to the beach they hatched on. This is where female turtles lay their eggs.

The places where animals make and produce their young are called breeding grounds.

Sea turtles are being affected by pollution. Turtles are eating plastic bags, thinking the plastic bags are jellyfish. Hatchlings are getting tangled in ropes and fishing nets that have washed up on beaches.

What can YOU do to stop pollution on beaches?

THE ADVENTURE OF THE ATLANTIC SALMON

Atlantic salmon start their lives in rivers. When they are three years old, the salmon migrate to the sea to eat and grow. However, they remember the river they started in.

As adults, the salmon journey back to the river they hatched in to spawn. There are often obstacles along the salmon's migration route. This makes reaching their destination harder.

Atlantic salmon spawning

Spawning usually happens in November and December.

Humans and human-made barriers can stop Atlantic salmon from reaching their breeding grounds. These barriers include dams and waterfalls. Fishing for salmon also stops the fish from completing their journey.

Many dams now have salmon ladders to help salmon cross them.

Once the salmon reach the river, they do not eat. Leaping over dams and dodging fishers uses lots of the salmon's energy. Many Atlantic salmon die once they have spawned.

THE HUMPBACK WHALE'S PASSAGE TO MOTHERHOOD

Humpback whales are seasonal migrators. This means they migrate to different places for summer and winter. One of those places is often their breeding grounds.

Humpback whales can swim over 4,350 miles (7,000 km) to reach their breeding grounds.

Female humpback whales usually give birth every two or three years. They normally only have one baby at a time. The mother and her baby stay together for up to a year.

Baby humpback whales are called calves.

The biggest threat to humpback whales is humans. Large ships often cross their migration routes. These ships can injure and sometimes kill humpback whales. This happens most when the whales are close to land.

Whale watching is a popular tourist activity. However, whale-watching boats can make humpback whales stressed. This affects mothers with calves the most. However, female humpback whales are very caring mothers, so most calves do reach adulthood.

Humpback whales can live for up to 90 years.

THE FLORIDA MANATEE FLOATS TO THE SPRINGS

Manatees are marine mammals. They have paddle-shaped tails and nails on the ends of their flippers. The nails show that manatees were land animals millions of years ago. Manatees migrate when the water gets cold.

Manatees usually live in rivers across the southern United States. In winter, when the water gets cold, the manatees gather in natural springs. Florida has many natural springs that stay warm throughout the year.

Natural springs are made when warm water from underground flows up to the surface.

Manatees need warm water to stay healthy. They do not have enough body fat to stay warm in cold water. In warmer months, manatees travel away from Florida. Sometimes they go as far as Texas or Massachusetts.

In summer, female manatees find quiet areas to give birth.

People have put safety measures in place to stop manatees from getting hurt during their migration. One safety measure is speed signs. These signs remind people to drive their boats slowly at certain times of year.

The police watch boating areas and create clear paths for manatees.

WHAT HAVE YOU LEARNED?

Let's see what you can remember about these aquatic animals that migrate? It is quiz time! Get your paper and pencil at the ready.

QUESTIONS

1. What are baby sea turtles called?

2. How old are Atlantic salmon when they migrate to the sea?

3. What is the biggest threat to humpback whales?

4. When do Florida manatees migrate back to Florida, summer or winter?

Answers:

1. Hatchlings
2. Three years old
3. Humans
4. Winter

GLOSSARY

DAMS	barriers that hold back the water in a river or stream
HABITAT	the natural home in which animals, plants, and other living things live
HATCH	when a baby animal comes out of its egg
MARINE MAMMALS	animals that live in or on the water, are warm-blooded, have a backbone, and produce milk
POLLUTION	harmful and poisonous things being added to an environment
PREDATORS	animals that hunt other animals for food
SPAWN	when a female salmon releases eggs so young can grow
TOURIST	a person visiting another place for fun

INDEX